An Anthology Of The Fowey River

by

Howard Alexander

Illustrated by

Klara Andersen

Fowey Rare Books
Cornwall PL23 1AR.

i

First Published by Fowey Rare Books 1995.
4 South Street, Fowey, Cornwall PL23 1AR.

© Howard Alexander 1995.

ISBN 1 899526 20 X

Printed in Great Britain by
Alexander Associates, Fowey.

A catalogue record for this book is available
from the British Library.

An Anthology

Of The

Fowey River

Introduction

The print accompanying this anthology is from a painting by au-
thor/artist *Klara Andersen*, who has lived, and at times, taught in
this area for over 35 years and who is related to the great *Hans
Christian Andersen*. The painting was made over a five month period (September 1994 through January 1995) and is the first time
that such a major work of the Fowey River has been attempted.
During the reign of Henry VIII, a chart/drawing was made (now
preserved in the British Museum and used in the Cornish section of
Lyson's *'Magna Britannia'*) which shows the Fowey River as seen
by the artist of the time. It is ludicrously out of scale but was the
only view available until now. The present painting is also a repre-
sentation and cannot claim geographic accuracy, but is neverthe-
less, an excellent attempt to show the main features of the navigable
part of the river. The foreground is a fair view looking due north,
whilst the top section is really more to the north west. The spatial
distances between features has of necessity been compressed.

The source of the Fowey River is near *Brown Willy* the highest
point in Cornwall on Bodmin Moor, and meanders over 30 miles of
moor and marsh to the Fowey Harbour and the sea. The *Fowey* is
tidal and navigable for small vessels from Lostwithiel Bridge, at
high tide, to Fowey Harbour about 7 miles south, and flows through
some of the most beautiful and historic countryside in the world.
Detailing interesting and prominent features from Lostwithiel to the
sea, the original of this painting hangs in Fowey Hall (see 14) and
measures 4ft x 3ft and prints of this painting can be found displayed

around the world. This book is concerned with the area of the painting, but there are many interesting and beautiful places just off the river that are not shown such as, Lanhydroc, Polkerris, Menabilly and the greater part of Polruan. Nearly all of the villages along the Fowey River have an annual Regatta which invariably includes some water activities.

The town of Fowey itself, has been important as a port since Celtic times. In the early centuries A.D., gold, mined in Southern Ireland, was transported by sea to the estuary of the river Camel and then hauled overland to Fowey. This was to avoid the dangers of Land's End and the Lizard. From Fowey, it was then exported to Europe and Egypt. The same route through Cornwall, was used by early missionaries and is part of what is known as the *'Saint's Way'*.

Today, Fowey is the 9th largest exporting port in the UK - mostly china clay - and also a major yachting centre, receiving more than 6,000 visiting yachts during the summer period. This represents over 30,000 extra visitors entering the town without a motor vehicle being involved, as they will mostly land at the pontoon on *Albert Quay*. This quay was so named after Queen Victoria landed here with Albert, the Prince Consort on September 8th 1846. The town is also well known for its writers such as *Sir Arthur Quiller-Couch*, known as *'Q'* (see 18), and *Dame Daphne du Maurier* (see 17). 'Q' wrote about Fowey in a number of his books, the most well known being *"The Astonishing History Of Troy Town"* (Troy being Fowey). Since the date of its first publication over 100 years ago, this story has amused a considerable succession of readers and time has in no way eroded its entertainment value.

Present writers are still producing stories related to Fowey, for example, the story of *Mary Bryant* as captured by *Judith Cook* in her book *"To Brave Every Danger"*. In 1786, Mary Bryant, a Fowey fisherman's daughter turned highway robber, was sentenced to hang for the theft of a silk hat and property worth 11 guineas. Her sentence was commuted to transportation to Australia and, after a barbarous nine-month voyage during which her first child was born, Mary arrived in Botany Bay where she married fellow convict William Bryant. Determined to escape her harsh sentence, Mary and William fled the penal colony in an open boat, sailing 3,254 miles in 69 days to the Dutch East Indies, only to be recaptured and brought back to London chained to the ship's deck in an open cage. Imprisoned in Newgate, and again threatened with death, her cause was championed by James Boswell, who was so taken with her at her trial, winning her first a reprieve, then a full pardon. Such is the stuff of this local girl, that MGM are proposing a film of this book in 1995 with locations in Fowey and Sydney, Australia.

Another Cornish author, *Denys Val Baker* lived at the Old Saw Mills near *Golant* in 1967, where he wrote *"Life Up The Creek"* and his wife *Jess*, started the *Mill Stream Pottery* in North Street in 1968. In 1939, *Leo Walmsley's "Love in the Sun"* was published, which tells how he and his wife had made a derelict army hut up Pont Creek, habitable and, how their furniture had been fashioned from driftwood. Daphne du Maurier wrote of this book: *"'Love In The Sun' will make other writers feel old fashioned. It is a revelation in the art of writing . . . Walmsley gives the reader a true story, classic in its simplicity . . . (the characters) are made of the very stuff of life itself."* Later, Walmsley wrote again from this old army hut and produced *"Paradise Creek"* and *"Sound Of The Sea"*. Many of these titles are scarce today. There are presently many writers and artists living in the area, as the surroundings evidently generate the right creative ambience.

There is a special class of boat that is sailed specifically in Fowey Harbour and around the immediate coast. Called 'Troys', they can be seen racing on the river from Easter time to the end of October. There are currently about 20 of these little yachts of which some of the fastest are built in Golant. Fowey also has a full-time RNLI Lifeboat which responds to many call-outs in life-threatening situations around our coast. On one occasion in 1990 when the then Prime Minister, Margaret Thatcher, made a visit to the Fowey lifeboat, she was invited for a 'spin around the harbour' which she readily accepted. During the trip a call was received from a distressed yacht and, there being no time to return the Prime Minister to shore, she went with the lifeboat on the call-out. A pump was put on board the distressed yacht, as she was taking in water from loose keel fastenings. The name of the yacht was *'Slipshod'*.

Much of the land around the estuary belongs to the *National Trust* which effectively preserves the landscape as seen today from further development. The whole area is a walkers paradise at all times of the year, and for those who prefer their exploring by boat, the water provides a unique means of viewing the estuary and upper reaches of the river during the warmer months.

The following descriptions of the features on the painting are numbered in sequence generally running from top left to bottom right of the painting.

An Anthology of the Fowey River

Main features of Painting
(see centre pages)

1. Lostwithiel.

The town charter dates back more than 800 years and Lostwithiel was the capital of Cornwall in the 13th century. The wealth of Lostwithiel was founded on the lucrative Cornish tin trade. Ironically, it was this same trade which caused the decline of the town, as the river Fowey silted up from tin waste flowing off Bodmin Moor.

The lovely old bridge dates from the 14th century and large sailing vessels once traded up to this point. Incredibly, it was only in 1939 that this ceased being the main road across the river and even today pedestrians use the *passing places* over the bridge piers, to allow traffic through, just as in the days of horse drawn vehicles. Today, in spite of the silting, shallow draught boats can still make the journey up river from Fowey. Most of the town is hidden from passing traffic as the main road skirts around the outer edge of the main centre. Part of the ruins of Lostwithiel Palace or, more correctly, the Great Hall of Lostwithiel, have been incorporated into the existing town. Built by Edmund, Earl of Cornwall in the XIII century, it housed the Parliament of Cornwall when Lostwithiel was the seat of government and the staple town

for tin in the county. *St Bartholomew's* Church is well known for its unusual lantern spire - unique in Cornwall - and dates from the 14th century. It was used as a refuge by Royalists in the Civil War. The font is more pagan than Christian. Made around the middle of the XIIIth century, it was given to the Church by a mayor of Lostwithiel. During the Civil War in 1644, the diarist 'Symonds' records: "In contempt of Christianity, Religion and the Church, they (*the Roundheads*) brought a horse to the font, and there, with their kind of ceremonies, did, as they called it, christen the horse and called him by the name of Charles in contempt of his Sacred Majesty". The damage caused during this period (and perhaps previously by agents of Henry VIII) has

defaced several of the carvings, but they are still intact enough to appreciate the various scenes and the stone masons craft. A Ley line is said to pass through the church entering at an angle from the south-west.

2. Restormel Castle

(Castel Rostormolgh).

First built before the development of Lostwithiel, around 1100 A.D., to control a crossing point of the river Fowey. The castle lost its strategic importance with the building of a bridge in the town but, Lostwithiel's growing prosperity at the time, led the Earls of Cornwall to move their centre of administration here from Launceston. Now a ruin, the Castle stands on ground that has been a fortification for probably a thousand years and is now part of *English Heritage*. It housed the Black Prince, the first Duke of Cornwall, in the 13th century and was recaptured from the Parliamentarians in the Civil War by Sir Richard Grenville in 1644 (the only time the castle saw any military action). From its highest part the Fowey can be viewed winding through the valley of Lanhydrock to the water meadows leading into Lostwithiel. The

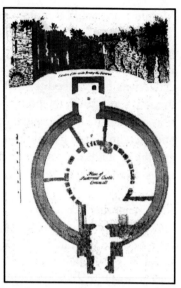

old protector of Lostwithiel, the castle ruins are preserved in beautiful, well kept surroundings and are well worth a visit.

3. Boconnoc
(Connoc's Dwelling or, Bo-Con-Oke - Place of Stunted Oaks)

3 miles east of Lostwithiel, Boconnoc can trace it's history back to the Normans. The estate and house were taxed in the Domesday Roll A.D. 1087. The first *recorded* owners were the De Cant family (1268) and in 1320-1386, the Manor was owned by the Carminows, latterly by Sir Oliver Carminow who married a daughter of Joan Holland (The Fair Maid of Kent), a grand-daughter of Edward I, who married the *Black Prince* as her second husband, for whom the *Duchy of Cornwall* was created.

Through the centuries, Boconnoc has been associated with many of this country's famous names and history-makers including Lord Russell, Earl of Bedford who sold Boconnoc in 1579 to Sir William

Mohun who rebuilt it. Later, Thomas Pitt purchased the estate with the proceeds of the famous Pitt Diamond which he sold to the Regent of France where it ended up in the hilt of Napoleon's sword. Pitt's grandson, William, became Prime Minister. Eventually, the estate was bequeathed to the Fortescue family who still own it although, since 1969, the house has not been lived in due to deterioration and subsidence. During the Second World War, Boconnoc House and the surrounding buildings were occupied by American troops and the grounds used as an ammunition dump in preparation for the invasion of Europe.

In the grounds (actually the largest park in Cornwall) can be seen the church, of which the dedication is unknown but was thought to have been consecrated in 1431. The most prominent monument in the park is the Obelisk which is 123 ft high and was erected in 1771 by Thomas Pitt, 1st Lord Camelford, in memory of his wife's uncle and benefactor, Sir Richard Lyttelton. It is situated between

Boconnoc and Braddock churches in the middle of an old military entrenchment near to where the *Battle of Braddock Down* was fought in the Civil War 1642 - 1646. During this period Boconnoc was

involved in two significant battles. In January 1643 the Parliament forces under Col. Ruthven impatiently attempted to enter Cornwall, which was strongly Royalist. The opposing forces met near Braddock Church, the Royalists being commanded by Bevil Grenville and Ralph Hopton (both subsequently knighted) marching from Boconnoc Park where they had bivouacked overnight. In a short time the Parliament forces were routed. A more important clash took place the following year, when the King's cause was beginning to wane. Lord Robartes of Lanhydrock (a 'sour Puritan') had indicated to the Earl of Essex, then commander-in-chief of the *Parliament Army*, that the Cornish were ready to surrender. Essex marched into the west, to be met by a strong force under Richard Grenville and Lord Goring and found he was pursued from the east by no less a person than the King with an army of several thousands. The King made his headquarters at Boconnoc and

the unfortunate *Roundheads* were gradually squeezed into Lostwithiel and Fowey, to their ultimate surrender at *Castledore*.

There are approximately 100 head of deer in the *Deer Park* contained within the grounds and also a garden of 20 acres which is open in the Spring for various charities. Boconnoc House and Park have been used for a number of film locations including the *BBC Poldark Series* and scenes from the 1993 film of *The Three Musketeers*.

4. Bradoc Church.

Believed to be a Cornish/Celtic corruption of Broad Oak, the Church of St Mary the Virgin at Bradoc (Braddock today) stands on a high hill amid beautiful green surroundings. The present building is 13th century and stands on the site of a former Church of which the Tower and the Norman arch leading into the Tower still remain. The Tower houses five bells, cast in 1845. The font is Norman and has four corner faces and large trees of life. Nearby, at Largin Farm are the trenches used by the Roundheads during the *Battle of Braddock Down*, whilst nearby, in Largin Wood, is Largin Castle - a camp or fort from the Iron Age. Also, near the village of West Taphouse, are 9 tumuli or barrows in three fields which are said to be the burial places of tribal kings. Bradoc Church was used for the wedding scene in the filming of Daphne du Maurier's "My Cousin Rachel".

5. Milltown Viaduct.

One of the many viaducts built in Cornwall last century and which were originally wooden constructions. This one was rebuilt in stone 100 years ago. The surrounding countryside is very pretty and romantic and one can well imagine Tristan and Isuelt walking here.

6. St Winnow Church.

Set in another beautiful river situation, this church stands on what was probably a 7th century Celtic monastery 500 years before the Conquest. It is mentioned in Domesday as *San Winnuc* and still has some remains of the Norman building. In the 15th century, the aisle and tower were added and the east windows are magnificent examples of glass craft and details much of the dress of the period. St Winnow Church is well known for its bench ends, carved from around 15th to 17th century and still in excellent condition. There is a plaque commemorating 2 parishioners who fought in the Zulu Wars and there are a number of South African connections with the church. Some scenes from the BBC *Poldark Series* were filmed here. Also at St Winnow can be seen a unique Farm Museum.

7. Lerryn.

A pretty fairytale village with swans, ducks, village green and many little boats. This is where Kenneth Grahame came for walks while he was writing "The Wind In The Willows" and the painting

shows a little dinghy along the creek leading to Lerryn with Badger, Mole and Ratty *'messing about in boats'*. This part of the Fowey River joins in with the Lerryn River with its source at Braddock. Before the second World War, sailing vessels travelled up here with

quarry stone. The river can be crossed by stepping stones at low tide and, at spring tides, can flood over the green and up to, and sometimes into, the surrounding cottages.
The bridge was rebuilt by order of
Queen Elizabeth I in 1573.

8. Golant - St Sampson's Church.

Golant is a small village devoted to boats, fishing and peace and quiet. Some of the famous *Troy* boats are built here. It has two historical connections that make it unique, that of the *The Life of St Sampson* and the story of *Tristan and Iseult*. The latter has many variations,one of which, goes as follows:

Tristan was a nephew of King Mark of Cornwall who was based at Castledore, and Iseult was an Irish princess betrothed to King Mark. Because of the hazards of travel in the 6th century Tristan was sent by his uncle to fetch Iseult. On the journey back from Ireland to Castledore she and Tristan fell in love and, inevitably, the human triangle was upset by the discovery of the lovers in compromising circumstances. Tristan fled to France where he was received with respect and he married the daughter of a local chief, another Iseult, but could not forget his first love. Wounded while hunting, he became seriously ill, and sent a ship to Cornwall with a message for Iseult to come to France to nurse him back to health. He instructed his sailors to hoist black

sails if their journey had been in vain, and white if she was aboard. His wife, discovering the plan, reported to Tristan that the sails were black whereas in fact they were white. Tristan died and, when Iseult arrived she too died and was buried beside her lover. Out of the graves grew two saplings, the branches of which became intertwined and it is said that *'in death they were united although parted in life'*.

The link with the church of St Sampson is that King Mark and Iseult made their devotions in state here, and that Iseult gave her best dress to the church.

St Sampson's life is one of the earliest recorded. He is known to have studied near Howth in Co. Dublin and later travelled to Wales and then to Cornwall where he established himself where the church now stands, having erected a shelter near the *Holy Well* which can be seen by the South Door. When he left Golant he went on to Brittany where he became Archbishop of Dol. The church is of traditional Celtic design and some parts are said to date from 1200 A.D. The present building was consecrated in 1509 and a restoration took place in 1842. There are five bells in the tower - the tenor dated 1807 weighs 6 cwt. There is interesting stained glass and much wood carving in the church.

9. Pavilion.

An inscription on this building refers to *Edward V* and, . . . the *Pleasure House*. It is thought to have been a signalman's house when the passenger trains passed here. It has recently been refurbished and today is an habitable folly.

10. St Cadix - Penpoll Creek.

An old Benedictine priory from the 12th century or earlier, set back from the main creek by a separate spur of water called St Cyric's. After dissolution in 1536 it was rented to a Bernard or Burcot Cranach, a German entrepreneur responsible for converting the 14th century flour mill at Lerryn as a smelting house for silver. The present building dates from around 1710. It is today owned by the Trevelyan family. Many swans inhabit this part of the Fowey River and

Penpoll Creek is an exquisite backwater ending up in Middle Penpoll.

11. Tristan Stone.

The plaque at this standing stone reads:

'**This stone erected nearby about 550 A.D. has on its north side a raised T, an early form of Christian cross. On its south side, in 6th century letters is inscribed:-**

**DRVSTANS HIC IACIT
CVNOWORI FILIVS**

Translated this reads "Tristan hear lies of Cunomorus the son".

Cunomorus was Marcos Cunomorus of the Medieval life of St Sampson and King Mark of Cornwall in the love story of Tristan and Iseult.' The T cross is called a *TAU* in Cornish.

An Anthology Of The Fowey River

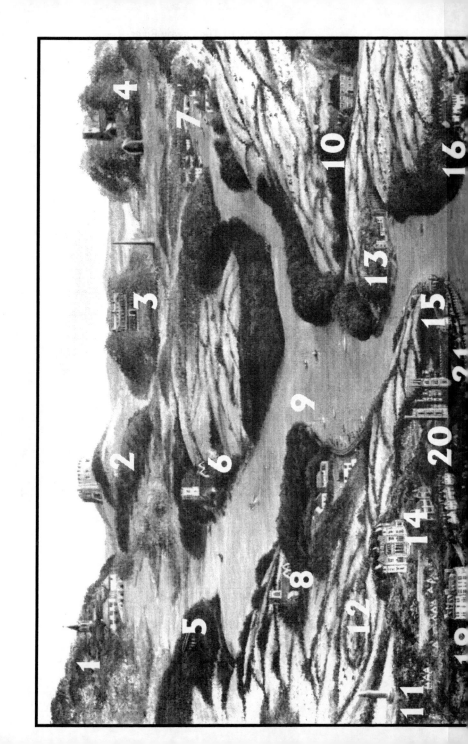

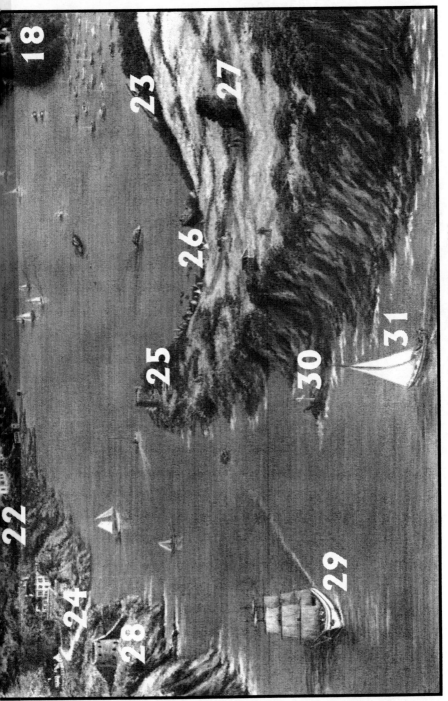

From an original painting by Klara Andersen 1995

12. Castledore.

The plaque at this site reads:

'**These earthworks, 225ft in diameter, enclosed a village dating from the 3rd to 1st centuries B.C.**

In the 6th century A.D. they surrounded the wooden hall of King Mark of Cornwall, who figures in the story of Tristan and Iseult and who is named on the stone found near here *(see 11)* **and now at the Four Turnings, Fowey. On 31st August 1644, the site was held by Parliamentary forces and taken by the Royalists.'**

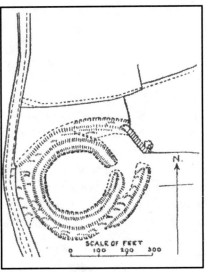

Some writers have identified *Castledore* as the *'Croftededor'* of Domesday Book and others think that Dore represents D'or, the gold colour found in the profusion of gorse bushes around the site (and indeed throughout Cornwall).

(If visiting this site, visitors should take care to enter only by the iron swing-gate at the proper entrance, as there is an electrified fence around the field at *Castledore* to keep grazing cattle contained.)

13. Mixtow.

A small hamlet named from the family 'Michelstowe' and corrupted to Mixtow and, the site of Kit's House, mentioned in 'Q's *"Astonishing History of Troy Town"*. This part of the river still has deep water but is completely sheltered from the prevailing winter weather and is a favourite spot for yachts escaping the gales which affect the lower harbour.

14. Fowey Hall.

An imposing 19th century residence built for Sir Charles Hanson, J.P., M.P., Sheriff and Lord Mayor of London. Fowey Hall was purchased by the *Countrywide Holidays* group in 1968 from the Hanson family. The building stands in more than 4 acres with commanding views over the harbour and sea. It is also well know for its association with *The Wind In The Willows* story by Kenneth Grahame, as he used it as *"Toad Hall"* in the story. (A careful scrutiny of the full colour print will result in a sighting of Mr Toad in his automobile!).

The original painting of *An Anthology Of The Fowey River* is currently on loan to Fowey Hall and can be viewed in their imposing entrance hall.

15. Clay Docks.

The china clay industry is Cornwall's most important source of revenue outside of tourism, with Fowey being the only harbour capable of loading deep water clay vessels. More than half of the clay shipped out of the county is loaded at these docks. In 1813 Joseph Austen of 'Place', had the harbour surveyed and built a quay and

 later a dock, to ship ore from his mines. A railway link was made in 1874 from Par to these docks, allowing china clay to be transported directly here for shipping for the first time. Prior to the first World War, Fowey experienced boom times as thousands of tons of clay was finding its way here to be shipped out via the docks on what became known as the *great white road* to Fowey. A ton of clay in those days fetched £1 per ton at source, as opposed to coal which realised less than half this amount. Most of the clay shipped out of Fowey today, is highly refined for paper coatings. Larger vessels are turned in the lower harbour and then reversed by the tugs, up river to the docks for loading.

16. Bodinnic.

A unique and pleasant way to enter or leave Fowey, is to take the Bodinnic vehicle ferry and cross the river. Bodinnic is on the east side of the river, and, a short steep climb up through the village

beyond 'The Ferry Inn', on the right-hand side, can be found the start of the *Hall Walk,* which takes you over Pont Creek and ends in Polruan, where a passenger ferry returns you to Fowey. Along this pathway will be found the 'Q' memorial *(see 18)* and at Pont, the old wharf is still there and is part of a delightful cottage which is now a National Trust property which can be rented for holidays.

17. Ferryside.

This is the *du Mauriers'* family home bought in 1927 and where *Daphne du Maurier* wrote her first book *'The Loving Spirit'* in 1928/9, (published in 1931). It is also where she met her future husband *Boy* Browning whom she married in 1932 and who was then a Major in the Grenadier Guards and later became Lieutenant-General Sir Frederick Browning. Daphne du Maurier was created a Dame of the British Empire in 1969. The house has, until recently, been lived in by Angela du  Maurier and is now occupied by Daphne du Maurier's son and his family. It was a boat-builders yard and had water running right through what is now an impressive sitting room, with magnificent views across the harbour out to the sea. The back wall of the house is the rock cliff face and has been incorporated marvellously into the house.

18. 'Q' Memorial on Hall Walk.

Sir Arthur Thomas Quiller-Couch was born at Bodmin in 1863, entered Trinity Collage Oxford in 1882 and started writing for the Oxford Magazine which was founded in 1883 and where he started using the pseudonym 'Q'. He was given a lectureship in 1886. Family financial difficulties forced 'Q' to move to London to work for the publishers Cassells and to write. His early novels were successful and in 1889 he married Louisa Amelia Hicks of Fowey. In six years he had paid off his father's debts, but overwork caused a breakdown and he was advised to leave London. Arthur and Louisa came home to Fowey in 1892. His health improved and he began to write again and became actively involved in local affairs ibecomimg Mayor, Vice President of the Fowey Royal Regatta, Commodore of the Yacht Club as well as holding other offices.

He was knighted in 1910 and received many honorary degrees and was given the freedom of Bodmin, Fowey and Truro. In 1912 'Q' was invited to become Edward VII Professor of English Literature at Cambridge. Here his lectures attracted larger audiences than any other at the university, and two collections of them were published - "On The Art Of Reading" in 1921 and, "On The Art Of Writing" in 1923. The latter is still in print! He always stressed that "Literature is not a mere science to be studied, but an art to be practised".

On the outbreak of war in 1914, 'Q' divided his time between Cambridge and Fowey. Sadly, with the advent of peace, his only son, Bevill, who had served in the army throughout the war, died in the influenza epidemic in 1919. 'Q' continued a prolific output of novels, short stories, literary criticism, serious and light verse, and children's books.

'Q' died at Fowey 19 May 1944 and was buried in the parish cemetery. For the next generation 'Q' left *"My little legacy of straight story-telling . . . I wish my books to be judged by themselves . . . they contain all of me that is worth preserving"*. He had a deep understanding of his country and its people. He was an academic of stature, a man of letters, and he was above all a Cornishman.

In 1945 a memorial fund was established in 'Q's honour. Grants from this fund have been made to those engaged in local research in literary or allied subjects.

19. Fowey Hotel.

Built in 1882, the hotel was used by 'Q' to deliver *"Literary Lectures"*. The gardens have been reinstated over the last few years and are a lasting memorial to landscaper Jim Buscombe, who died in 1994. They are well worth a visit as the lower section is now used as a Tea Garden with stunning views over the harbour. Noel Coward stayed here as well as a string of other well-known personalities.

20. Place House.

The Treffry family association with 'Place' (Cornish for palace) goes back to the late 13th century and, an eighth generation Treffry (John) was knighted by Edward, the Black Prince, at Crecy in 1346. The present building in essence, dates back to 1457 when, in a reprisal for raids on the French coast by local seamen, Fowey was attacked by the French in 1456 and set on fire. They were repulsed at 'Place' by Elizabeth Treffry, who is reputed to have had lead poured over the attackers. Joseph Austen, 1782-  1850, of the Treffry family, was a great industrialist who was responsible for creating Par Harbour in an effort to save Fowey from the ravages of the ore being transported from his mines to the waiting ships here. He also constructed canals and the Luxulyan viaduct/aqueduct. The Treffry family still live here and have been involved in the growth of the town in many ways including the china clay industry and other developments. The house and grounds are occasionally opened for charitable functions.

21. St Fimbarrus.

This ancient church is dedicated to St Finn Barr, who was the first Bishop of Cork, Ireland (A.D. 613 - 630). On a pilgrimage to Rome, possibly for his consecration, he crossed the sea following the old trade and pilgrim route to Padstow (north coast of Cornwall) overland to Fowey and from here via Brittany to Rome. During his stay in Fowey, he *'built a little church in a sheltered place between the hills'*.

St Finn Barr's Church replaced an earlier one, that of St Goran (or Guron) who, probably left his cell at Bodmin when St Petroc arrived, established a church at Fowey and finally settled at Goran. (Celtic Christianity was an influence in Cornwall long before Roman missionaries arrived in Britain in A.D. 597).

About A.D. 1150, a Norman Church was built here but unfortunately only the font has survived. At this stage, the Church at Fowey was served by Benedictine monks from Tywardreath Priory (a few miles away) and a resident vicar was appointed in 1260. In 1328, the Church was rebuilt as a result of destruction possibly by pirates, and it was dedicated in 1336 by the Bishop of Exeter, to St Nicholas of Bari, patron saint of sailors, but the name failed to replace that of St Finn Barr.

In 1456, the Church was partially destroyed (this time by the French) and restoration began again in 1460 with the help of the Earl of Warwick, Lord High Admiral of England, and lasted until the next century. The tower, wagon roof, rood screen and loft date from this period. Warwick's badge (the ragged staff) can be seen on the second string course of the Church Tower. Around 1500, the Treffry brothers undertook to widen the narrow south aisle and extend it to make a family chapel and the clerestory windows, unusual for Cornwall, were constructed.

In 1876, an important restoration took place removing the western gallery, providing a new roof for the north aisle, a clergy vestry, choir stalls and pews for the congregation. A choir vestry was added in 1894. The font, survivor from the Norman Church, is made of hard elvan from a quarry near Padstow. The uncarved portion is thought to be unfinished because the carver died. The pulpit was made in 1601 from the panelling of the captain's cabin of a Spanish Galleon.

On a pew near the second pillar on the south side, there is a memorial to 'Sir Arthur Quiller-Couch who lived at "The Haven" on the Esplanade'. (see 22). There are also some ancient brasses of the Treffry and Rashleigh families, the former dating from 1456. Kenneth Grahame, author of "The Wind In The Willows" was married here in 1899 and many of the scenes in his book were based on the River Fowey.

22. The Haven.

Built around 1875, this was the home of Sir Arthur Quiller-Couch from the time of his departure from London in 1892, until his death in 1944.

"I can't afford a mile of sward
Parterres and peacocks gay
For velvet lawns and marble fauns
Mere authors cannot pay.

And so I went and pitched my tent
Above a harbour fair
Where vessels picturesquely rigged
Obligingly repair . . . "

The building itself has no special architectural features but has been listed because of the association with 'Q'. It had a wonderful copper kitchen that is remembered by some locals. Many famous writers were guests at The Haven including Kenneth Grahame and Daphne du Maurier. This part of the Esplanade was known as the

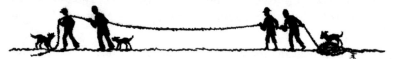

Rope Walk as it had the perfect geometry for rope-making in the days of sailing ships.

23. Brazen Island.

Originally an isolated rock (hence the name) which is now incorporated into the main building, which was a sardine factory in 1883 but liquidated shortly after in 1887 (presumably through the lack of sardines). The Freehold of the factory was purchased by the Fowey Harbour Commissioners in 1926. The transition from sail to steam and later, diesel engines, created the need for an engineering works and from this time, the present complex, slipway and works was gradually built. The *Lantic Bay* Dredger was built here in 1953 and is still working full time.

24. Readymoney Cove.

Romantically associated (without any substantial evidence) with smugglers. Readymoney is a delightful beach overlooked by the Rashleigh house at Point Neptune built around 1865, and an old lime kiln which today shares duties as a public toilet facility and a pump-house. There are steps up from the beach (at low tide) to the cliff leading to St Catherine's Castle or, at high tide, the castle can be reached by the cliff path behind, which also leads to *'Loves Lane'*, a National Trust path which takes you for a climb through the woods to the upper part of Fowey.

25. Blockhouse.

This blockhouse is comparatively well preserved due to the efforts of various enthusiastic councillors and conservationists on the Polruan side of the river. There were two (the Fowey side being ruined beyond hope) which were built end of the 14th century to

protect the harbour from pirates and the French. A chain was pulled up across the river between the two blockhouses to stop vessels entering the harbour and conversely, to stop them leaving if they had the temerity to "cross the line".

26. Polruan.
A very old fishing village and where most of the fishing boat-building took place (and today there is still an active boat yard, building and repairing boats of all types). It is said that St Ruan was the

first to occupy the top of Polruan Hill, which is where St Saviours ruin stands today. Polruan is very steep and well protected from the prevailing winds and Polruan Pool is a haven for small boats. Polruan is part of the parish of Lanteglos-by-Fowey and many of the residents are artists and writers who are attracted to the quiet nature of the village. The Polruan Ferry crosses the river to Fowey every 15 minutes every day of the year and is still the best way in and out of the village, as the alternative is either a drive to the Bodinnic Ferry or via Lostwithiel, a 40 minute journey.

27. St Saviours Ruin.

Standing high on the hill overlooking Polruan, St Saviours chapel was built long before any of the surrounding churches and dates from the 8th century. The remaining buttress indicates that the chapel was solidly built and was a prominent landmark for ships. It would have been a good lookout point for checking on approaching enemy vessels and the first monks would have been effective coastguards providing a warn-

ing by ringing the chapel's bells. St Saviours was enlarged by Sir Richard Edgcumbe in 1488.

28. St Catherine's Castle.

Built by Henry VIII who had cannons placed here to defend the town from French invaders. It appears in many drawings of Fowey Harbour. The name comes from a chapel built nearby dedicated to St Catherine, which was dissolved by Henry VIII and parts of it  were probably used in constructing the castle. The Rashleigh Mausoleum now stands on the old chapel site.

29. Maria Asumpta.

A living piece of maritime history and heritage, this is the oldest wooden square-rigged sailing ship in the world still sailing. She was built near Barcelona in 1858 and traded between the Argentine, Brazil and Mediterranean until the turn of the century, when she was sold and operated from SE Spain and traded with N. Africa and Nova Scotia for the codfish schooners. She has since been to the Caribbean, Canada and the Great Lakes and, crossing the Atlantic in 1988, created a record for such an old vessel. She is today operated by a trust, "The Friends of Maria Asumpta" and often calls at Fowey where she was overhauled at Brazen Island in 1994.

30. Punche's Cross
(or Paunches, Pontius, Ponts, or the French 'Ponce' Cross)

Lying at the eastern tip of the Fowey River below the cliffs to the south-west of St Saviours Point, this cross is said to be associated with Pontious Pilate as well as Jesus' uncle, Joseph of Arimethea, who it is said passed this way with the young Jesus to inspect his tin mines. It is marked on very early charts and if the cross was damaged by storms, it was reinstated by monks from Tywardreath. It is today under the responsibility of the Fowey Harbour Commissioners. The true origin of the name is unknown but it *may* be a corruption of Pontius. Whatever its real history, it is an important warning, as when the tide is high, only the top of the cross is visible, indicating that there are some very dangerous rocks below!

31. Yacht Crescendo.

Built in 1975 in Cape Town, this 39ft yacht was placed in the first *Cape to Rio Race* in 1976, from where she went to the Mediterranean before sailing back to Cape Town in 1978. The present owners bought her in 1980 and sailed her to Europe via Brazil, the Caribbean, USA and the Azores, eventually mooring up in Fowey in October 1983, since when she has been a local landmark, occasionally chartering around the coast here. The flag at her stern is the St Piran or Cornish flag.